ONCE UPON A DREAM

Fantastic Verse

Edited By Lynsey Evans

First published in Great Britain in 2024 by:

Young Writers
Remus House
Coltsfoot Drive
Peterborough
PE2 9BF
Telephone: 01733 890066
Website: www.youngwriters.co.uk

Printed and bound in the UK by BookPrintingUK
Website: www.bookprintinguk.com
YB0588N

FOREWORD

Welcome Reader, to a world of dreams.

For Young Writers' latest competition, we asked our writers to dig deep into their imagination and create a poem that paints a picture of what they dream of, whether it's a make-believe world full of wonder or their aspirations for the future.

The result is this collection of fantastic poetic verse that covers a whole host of different topics. Let your mind fly away with the fairies to explore the sweet joy of candy lands, join in with a game of fantasy football, or you may even catch a glimpse of a unicorn or another mythical creature. Beware though, because even dreamland has dark corners, so you may turn a page and walk into a nightmare!

Whereas the majority of our writers chose to stick to a free verse style, others gave themselves the challenge of other techniques such as acrostics and rhyming couplets.

Each piece in this collection shows the writers' dedication and imagination – we truly believe that seeing their work in print gives them a well-deserved boost of pride, and inspires them to keep writing, so we hope to see more of their work in the future!

CONTENTS

All Saints CofE Primary School, Wandsworth

Maya Todorov (10)	1
Bea Bowden (10)	2
Georgie Gough (10)	3
Ronnie Lynch (10)	4
Anais Ryan (10)	5

Appleton Wiske CP School, Appleton Wiske

Beatrix Dyke (11)	6
Oliver Brooks (8)	7
William Ferrie (9)	8
Lily Easby (10)	9
Maddy Turner (9)	10
Dylan Bateson (8)	11
Rupert Robinson (8)	12
Noah Jake (9)	13
Max Barrett (8)	14
Bella Sygrove (8)	15
Arthur Turner (7)	16

Clyst Hydon Primary School, Clyst Hydon

Aurora (8)	17
Polly Wooltorton-Renouf (9)	18
Ayonthea Mariner-Parr (11)	19

Garelochhead Primary School, Garelochhead

Alice Kirk (10)	20
Blake Mitchell (10)	21
Oscar Campbell (10)	22
Maggie Callan (10)	23
James Graham (10)	24
Cody Beck (11)	25
Amy McGuire (10)	26
Anne Pizarro Griffiths (10)	27
Helen Pizarro Griffiths (10)	28
George Chapman (10)	29

Great Bedwyn CE Primary School, Great Bedwyn

Delaney Harris (9)	30
Reuben Rubanko-Crook (9)	31
Daisy Hounslow (9)	32
Poppy Drew (9)	34
Eddie Yorke (9)	35
Max Wilsey (9)	36
Jessica Green (8)	37
Harper Griffin (8)	38
Oliver Mendus-Edwards (8)	39
Jess Leslie (9)	40
Sophie Brown (8)	41
Max Culmer (8)	42
Jake Levin (8)	43
Charlie Crees (9)	44
Tally	45

Holy Cross Catholic Primary School, South Ockendon

Chichebem Biachi (11)	46
Dromoh Hammond (9)	47
Cianne Osei (10)	48
Ella McNaughton (9)	49
Eliana Atanda (9)	50
Elsabeth Yeates (9)	51
Akintoyese Akinnunmé (8)	52
Ruby Moore (8)	53
Rayn Zivarattinam (10)	54
Alexander Valencia Ferreira (10)	55
Samuel Kinuthia Mburu (8)	56
Melissa Valencia Ferreira (10)	57
Otitodilichukwu Jibunoh (9)	58

Kirkhill Primary School, Kincorth

Cole Smith (11)	59
Michael Ziedins (12)	60
Jai McGowan (11)	62
Kiara Haviarova (11)	63
Oliver Ziedins (12)	64
Harley Sutherland (11)	65
Tyler Wallace (11)	66
Laci Forsyth (11)	67
Mason MacDonald (11)	68
Ava Slatter (11)	69

Lister Junior School, Tuebrook

Seth Hendry (9)	70
Harry Murney (10)	71
Nathan Kidd (10)	72
Joanna Tom (9)	73
Eva Barnes (9)	74
Scarlett Rutland (10)	75
Amelia Sarki (10)	76

Little Parndon Primary Academy, Harlow

Nicole Golebiewska (11)	77
Laura Macovei (11)	78

Toby Wilsher (10)	80
Tegan Knowles (10)	81
Paris Gibson (11)	82
Emilie Sims (10)	83
Zoha Awan (10)	84
Harry Cockman (11)	85
Evie Mary-Jean Yeo (11)	86
James Patten (10)	87

Mendell Primary School, Bromborough

Adrija Das Gupta (10)	88
Amber-Rose Philpott (10)	89
Emma Scott (10)	90
Archie Williams (9)	91
George Lloyd (9)	92
Grace Lavinia Gladwin (10)	93
Emily Henshaw (9)	94

Pilgrim Primary Academy, Plymouth

Sarah Tekle (11)	95
Alison Oldfield (11)	96
Sienna Newton (9)	97
Joyce Lopes (10)	98
Edlyn Hayfron-Taylor (11)	99
Arsema Muluebirhan (11)	100
Lacey Williams (10)	101
Lola-Rose Wilson (10)	102
Marcus Wang (11)	103
Jan Grzybowski (11)	104
Sophia Jobbins (11)	105
Gabrella Oshilim (8)	106
Hollie Goff (10)	107
Scarlett Bailey (8)	108
Alya Mohammed (9)	109
Aisha Akanji (10)	110
Phoebe Hepburn-Phillips (11)	111

St Bartholomew's Primary School, Glasgow

Frankie McGuire (10)	112
Quinn Brogan (9)	113
Mollie French (10)	114
Freya Molloy (10)	115
Kamsiyochukwu Joshua Uzor (10)	116
Iyanuoluwa Oni (10)	117
Winifred Ubah (11)	118
Stephen Ross (10)	119
Ella-Mae O'Brien (9)	120
Zoey McLaren (10)	121
Braxton James (10)	122
Kacey McCallion (10)	123
Noah Sisawo (10)	124

St George's Primary School, Portland

Layla Gorman (10)	125
Grace Peters-Daw (9)	126
Holly-Jean McAllister-Naylor (9)	128
Lillie Laing (9)	129
Willow-Rose Day (10)	130
Skylar Conlan (10)	131
Matilda Fairman (9)	132
Ella Ward (9)	133
Emily Woodcock (10)	134
Imogen Burley (10)	135
Isobel Comben (10)	136
Isla Porter-Bargery (10)	137
Orla White (9)	138
Kiahola-Joan Coker (10)	139
Xander Hibell (9)	140
Micah Lively (9)	141
Charlie Matterface (10)	142
JJ Porter Cross (10)	143
Lois Westwood (10)	144
Maisie Norris (9)	145
Ruby Hicks (9)	146
Noah Flavell (9)	147
Phoebe Wilson (10)	148
Maddie Carney (10)	149

Jax Moore (9)	150
Annabel Barnes (10)	151
Dominic Gault (9)	152
Demi-Lola Roberts (9)	153
Ruby Grant Jones (9)	154
Paige Coleman (9)	155

Woodhouse Primary Academy, Quinton

Jeron Harrison (10)	156
Lilly Keenahan (11)	158
Rawnaq Azad (10)	159
Sagaa Abo Arida (11)	160
Joseph Clerkin (10)	161

Woolton Primary School, Woolton

Ella Dyce (10)	162
Yu Chen Xu (10)	164
Sadie Weeks (10)	166

THE POEMS

In My Head

In my head, I see a world of bright and new,
Where the fun never ends and the lights never dim,
Rainbows soar in the deep blue skies,
And there are never races you can't win.

At one point my head is spinning,
As I look around this unknown place,
I'm a bird, white wings and clawed feet,
Soaring above the mountain peaks!

Suddenly, just as I'm getting used to it,
Ping! What is this place?
I'm an astronaut exploring the galaxy,
Moonwalking across planets,
Staring into deep space.

What's that I hear?
Yet another ping!
As all those dreams pass by me,
I'm a vet, an explorer, a pilot, a swimmer,
A gymnast, a skydiver, a singer, a winner!

Maya Todorov (10)
All Saints CofE Primary School, Wandsworth

The Portal

A dream is the most magical place,
You can be anything, anyone, have any face.

Father Christmas, a great white shark,
A flying dancer, or Noah on his ark.

All of these I have been when I've snuggled down to dream.

I have seen wondrous dimensions, dangerous seas,
Unicorns and fairies, even pirate dogs and fleas.

A whole world of wonder just there in my bed,
Billions of ideas crammed in my head.

What would life be if we didn't dream?
A dull grey world with no colourful beam.
So get tucked in and close your eyes,
To prepare for tonight's amazing surprise.

Bea Bowden (10)
All Saints CofE Primary School, Wandsworth

Portal Of Your Mind

Your mind is a portal you go through every night,
So just lie back and let your mind take flight.

To a fairy tale gone wrong,
Where you're pursued by witches,
That suddenly are gone,
Turned into giant marshmallows,
That are just out of reach.

You are like a computer that has been hacked,
And is out of control,
Trapped in an arcade game under attack,
Fighting your mind,
To escape the greedy ghost.

Your mind is a portal you go through every night,
If you have a nightmare, be ready to fight.

Georgie Gough (10)
All Saints CofE Primary School, Wandsworth

The Hero Child

While I lie in bed,
Deep in REM,
I take my place,
I need to score this pen!
The pressure is on,
I start to fret,
This ball must get into the back of the net,
The crowd goes silent,
I must kick this ball hard and violent,
I pull my leg back, ready to swing,
Whoosh! Goes the ball,
Yes! Top bins,
Cheering and chanting supporters go wild,
My dream, I become the hero child.

Ronnie Lynch (10)
All Saints CofE Primary School, Wandsworth

In My Dreams Every Night

With spiders flying through the sky,
I try to hide from the monsters lurking through my eyes,
While I cry, I write this poem to you,
So you too don't get stuck in this horrible dream,
Get me out, get me out please,
Then I realise I'm in my bed,
And all those monsters were in my head.

Anais Ryan (10)
All Saints CofE Primary School, Wandsworth

Dream World

In my dream world is a wonderful place,
All the dogs and cats are running a race,
In my dream world, everyone is happy,
And none of the tiny dogs are yappy,
There is a small fennec fox, tall and proud,
When I see her, I feel like screaming out loud,
The fennec fox is my favourite animal,
But close behind is the springer spaniel.

In my dream world, money grows on trees,
And everywhere around are beautiful bees,
Money falls on the hard, soft ground,
Because it's so light, you can't hear a sound,
It is scary sometimes in my dream world,
You see, at night, everything gets whirled,
There are clowns and spiders around my house,
Whilst in the corner sits a scared mouse.

In the morning, the birds begin to tweet,
The sun kindly heats up the cold street.

Beatrix Dyke (11)
Appleton Wiske CP School, Appleton Wiske

Rich Footballer

I play for City,
I play up front, it is so easy,
There is no pity for City.

Last year we won the title, it was hard at first,
But I swish past the defenders,
And when the ball is on me, it is goal after goal after
goal.

I can't stop putting it in the net,
And I am dodging with a crash.
No one is richer than me.

I own half of the world,
I have a money machine.
I have expensive cars.
I have a casino and helpers and a football pitch.

I am so rich,
And I have ten football statues at my house.
I am City's best player.

And I have a statue,
And in my house I have a big pool,
And I have a professional chef.

Oliver Brooks (8)
Appleton Wiske CP School, Appleton Wiske

Rich Life

Mansions are as big and expensive as Lamborghinis and Ferraris.
And my Lamborghini is as fast as lightning.
Four of my children have their own houses and servants.
No one is as rich as me.
I am the richest man in the world.
Singers are making a new song called Love You.
I love my children and wife so much.
I give them so much security and servants.
One of my children has got an iPhone 15.
No one owns as many Lamborghinis as me because I own 500 million.

William Ferrie (9)
Appleton Wiske CP School, Appleton Wiske

Shark Chase

The ocean is clear,
I'm all alone,
How did I get here?
Where is my home?

The never-ending ocean,
In front of my eyes,
Something's approaching me,
There's red in the skies.

The palm trees are dancing,
The fish all escape,
The tip of a fin,
Draped in seagrape.

The waves are troops,
Competing in a battle,
Gosh that's a shark,
Not horses and cattle.

Lily Easby (10)
Appleton Wiske CP School, Appleton Wiske

Joy

Laughing with joy
Painting the sky
Stars are flashing
Wiggling my toes.

Who knows
Bang, crash, whoosh
Wolf dances in the night
Giggling like bells.

Bursting with colour
Whizz, fizz, sparkle
Turning into a star
Twinkle, twinkle.

Red as a ruby
Pretty as a princess
Daydreaming
Fluffy like a teddy.

Maddy Turner (9)
Appleton Wiske CP School, Appleton Wiske

My Dream Footballer

I am strong as a rock
As deadly as a T-rex
I play for Liverpool
I am a defender
I live in a big mansion
I can block big shots
I am from the Netherlands
I have won the Champions League
I am one of the greatest defenders
I am as fast as lightning
I score 100 goals per season.

Have you guessed it yet?

Answer: Virgil van Dijk.

Dylan Bateson (8)
Appleton Wiske CP School, Appleton Wiske

My Dream Footballer

I'm as fast as lightning,
As strong as a horse,
As precious as gold,
I score 200 goals a year,
I play football,
I play for Man City,
I don't play striker,
I play left wing,
I like singing,
I wear bracelets,
I never miss,
Have you guessed who I am yet?

Answer: I'm Jack Grealish.

Rupert Robinson (8)
Appleton Wiske CP School, Appleton Wiske

Lost In A Forest

Going to bed,
And waking up,
In a dark misty forest,
With lonely mammoth-sized trees.
Clowns coming and crows flying,
Gunshots heard, no signs of a bird.
Crunches! And crackles! And creepy crawlies crawling,
Ghosts running towards me as fast as lightning,
Waking up and realising it was a dream.

Noah Jake (9)
Appleton Wiske CP School, Appleton Wiske

The World Of Cats!

Bow down to Queen Sasha,
Or she'll take all of your kitty toys,
She'll take your kitty seat,
The girls and the boys,
Sash will attack,
And will recruit a pack,
Siberian kittens,
Tabby cats too,
Stay very alert,
Or she will pounce on you!

Max Barrett (8)
Appleton Wiske CP School, Appleton Wiske

The Magical Unicorn

U nder the water, it floats gracefully

N uts are its favourite food

I nvisible like a ghost

C reature that is magical

O n its head it has a flowing mane

R ainbow coloured fur

N ight and day, it dances across the land.

Bella Sygrove (8)

Appleton Wiske CP School, Appleton Wiske

The Sky Flash

The flying giant,
Flapping with lines on its wings,
It flies super fast like a rocket,
It flies really well,
With an angry attitude,
It is as tall as a bear,
It is as fast as a Ferrari,
What is it?

Answer: It is Charizard.

Arthur Turner (7)
Appleton Wiske CP School, Appleton Wiske

The Gorm

T errifying eyes

H uge steel armour

E very fear comes to me

G hastly

O n my bed, I am tiny compared to The Gorm

R un as fast as you can, they'll still catch you

M any times they'll find you but you'll run away.

Aurora (8)

Clyst Hydon Primary School, Clyst Hydon

Bat-Bots

B at-bots are *evil*
A nd very very weird
T hey shoot dark red-blue lasers

B at wings, and a cone robot body
O dd, eight legs
T he bat-bots are black with gold swirls
S uddenly they're all in a dream.

Polly Wooltorton-Renouf (9)
Clyst Hydon Primary School, Clyst Hydon

My Dream

M any weeks at sea
Y elling.

D anger creeps closer,
R ifles shooting,
E nemies approaching.
A live?... No, dead.
M ay the odds be in your favour...

Ayonthea Mariner-Parr (11)
Clyst Hydon Primary School, Clyst Hydon

The Nightmare...

This dream is about a monster that has purple spikes
on its back!
Eyes as red as lava,
Black skin as dark as the darkest room,
And sharp shark teeth which gleam as bright as the
sun.
It's like it tried to kill me in my dream,
Running as fast as I could.
Suddenly there was a loud, huge *bang!*
Coming from the entrance door. It was cold.
It felt like the North Pole, it was so cold.
Then I woke up, but it was pitch black like I was still
asleep in a cave!
But I was sleeping upstairs in my room,
No on the cold floor in a cave.
At 3am it all happened again at the same time and on
the same day of the week.
I was so scared to death. It happened every Saturday,
always at 3am exactly.
Then it killed me for once and it was real.
It wasn't a dream at all!

Alice Kirk (10)
Garelochhead Primary School, Garelochhead

The Smiler

T he thrilling sight of The Smiler in front of me,
H earing the taunting laughs, I'm buzzing like a bee.
E xcitedly, I climb into the cart, then *boom* - my dad ruins it by letting out a fart!

S till can't believe I'm here, about to embrace fear.
M y dreams are about to come true; come on The Smiler, let's see it through!
I mpressively, the powerful Smiler slowly climbs the lift hill; now it's ready to drop.
L aughing my head off, I don't want it to ever stop,
E ntering the second lift hill, everyone is laughing, it's such a thrill!
R oller coaster, roller coaster, you make me feel so free. The Smiler comes to an end, as sad as you can be.

Blake Mitchell (10)
Garelochhead Primary School, Garelochhead

The Upside-Down World

It's upside down in dreamland,
The green grass in the sky,
Mixed with the clear blue sea,
And the clouds below our feet,
Stars twinkling all around the floor,
As we stand on the clouds,
The trees dance from above,
As the birds give us a stare,
My dog and I lie in the air.

The red roses are doing cartwheels in the air,
My dog, the birds and I all give each other a glare,
As we look across, we see a sharp tool, like a needle
hook,
We follow the hook, and it leads us to a house,
That is made of cake with a candy cane frame, a door
made of fudge and windows made of sugar glass.

It's an upside-down world in my dream!

Oscar Campbell (10)
Garelochhead Primary School, Garelochhead

The Midnight Bang

One dark midnight,
When I went to sleep,
I heard something that started to creep,
Through my parents' room and from the back door,
It passed my brother's bedroom and opened my door.

I pretended to sleep as the floor started to creak,
I shivered and shook as I could sense my fear,
As it walked out of my room and slammed the door,
I sat back up with no realisation.

It crept back in as fast as a flash,
I didn't even notice,
It scared me with a loud bang,
Throwing me back down on my bed,
Then, with all the shock,
I had finally awoke,
Suddenly realising, I drank a little bit of coke!

Maggie Callan (10)
Garelochhead Primary School, Garelochhead

Candy World

Every night in my dreams,
There is a magnificent candy world!
Me and my friends watching the house with lots of
steam coming out,
Rainbow drops as the windows and a curled toffee
spire.

It was a gingerbread house, inside lived a gingerbread
man, wife and child,
With a dog as small as a sprout!
Candy canes make a tasty gate as they dance around,
Inside it was as hot as a fire,
There was a great big *bang* sound!

It was a big party with all the chocolate mice!
Then I woke up and it disappeared,
Perhaps it will come back and visit another year!
Every night in my dreams.

James Graham (10)
Garelochhead Primary School, Garelochhead

Dark, Dark Days

It was in the morning when I was up.
I got ready but the light was dark like the night sky,
My legs were thin,
Even thinner than a bin!
I scrambled for the door, not knowing what was ahead.
Now don't get me started, but the bed was full of *lead!*
Outside, the trees were flowing angrily in the wind.
Suddenly, a shadow appeared.
It gave chase, it felt like a race!
My heart was pounding like a kangaroo.
I had a sudden feeling to go to the loo...
Bang! Boom!
And then I went to the loo.
Suddenly, the mysterious shadow went *boo!*

Cody Beck (11)
Garelochhead Primary School, Garelochhead

25

Nightmares

N othing in the room that I knew,

I took a step and saw so many spiders,

G iant ones, small ones and poisonous ones too,

"**H** elp me!" I screamed, but no one could hear me!

T he room started to shrink with a *bang!*

M y mum, I wish I could see,

A mazingly, a platform arose and danced into the moon with a *whoosh!*

R eally high into the sky, higher and higher,

E ven higher than the moon,

S uddenly I woke up in my bed terrified.

Amy McGuire (10)
Garelochhead Primary School, Garelochhead

The Love Of A Child For Her Mother

The child ran into the woods,
Knowing that this was her mum's favourite spot,
She felt lonely, like not having her best friend by her side.

She saw a sparkly red button on a tree in front of her,
Shining as bright as the northern star,
She clicked on it,
She fluttered like a butterfly up to the clouds.

She saw cotton candy and licked it,
She saw her mum with open arms,
A teddy bear behind her,
She hugged it.

She woke up knowing that her mum would never leave her side.

Anne Pizarro Griffiths (10)
Garelochhead Primary School, Garelochhead

Dreaming Of My BFF

My lamb is my best friend,
I wonder where she is now.
I cry for her every night before I go to bed.
My dad knows how much it hurts!

In my dreams I still hear her little hooves clopping on
the grass,
I wish she was here,
I know she is gone.
I miss her,
I so wish she was here!

Helen Pizarro Griffiths (10)
Garelochhead Primary School, Garelochhead

Once Upon A Dream

In my dreams every night
I dream of a dream
That I've never dreamed
Before with cocks and
Crows and rowing
Boats and places
That I've never
Been before
With a sun
As hot as a
Blazing fire
I'm going
To be in a
Choir!

George Chapman (10)
Garelochhead Primary School, Garelochhead

My Dreams

I am not a daydreamer
But when I say goodnight
It takes me to another world
With my eyes shut tight.

I dream of skiing down the piste
Face planting in the snow
I will get better every day
As down the hill I go.

Sometimes I swim with dolphins
Leaping through the waves
I dive down deeper than I should
I know the pod will save.

Sometimes I run with champions
With legs that run so fast
I don't give up, I win the race
As everyone I've passed.

When morning comes, eyes open wide
Those things I dreamed may go
One day soon I'll get there
I'll try my best I know.

Delaney Harris (9)
Great Bedwyn CE Primary School, Great Bedwyn

The Cup

I'm on the halfway line with my team,
For tonight's amazing dream,
It's time for us to all be bold,
To win the trophy made of gold.

For Brazil up comes Neymar,
Who blasts the ball over the bar,
Now it's 4-3, now it's all on me,
To lead us on to victory,

Just one kick away from glory,
I walk up to the ball nervously,
I take the ball and get myself set,
As I strike the ball into the back of the net.

I run back to join my team,
This must be a dream,
Sixty years are in the past,
Football's coming home at last!

Reuben Rubanko-Crook (9)
Great Bedwyn CE Primary School, Great Bedwyn

The Monster Who Came To My Place

One dark, wet night,
As I had fallen asleep,
There was no sound, not even a squeak,
Suddenly, there was a creak.

It came from up the stairs,
I hoped it was my mum
With her pink, soft flares.

A few minutes later,
It creaked one more time,
I thought I was going
Out of my mind!

I felt some wind on my face,
But there was no evidence
Of the monster who came to my place.

I heard him eat a packet of toffees
I got them when my mum
Was getting her coffee.

I knew the monster wouldn't go,
So let the monster sleep till it was day.

Daisy Hounslow (9)
Great Bedwyn CE Primary School, Great Bedwyn

Flying High

In the sky I fly above,
With my magical heart of love.
The clouds are made of cotton candy,
My owl eyes are quite so handy.
I spot the sun and when I'm done,
I carry on with my dream all day,
And in my class I will soon say,
"I have got magic powers,
I always carry my beautiful flowers."
In the sky I feel free,
Because when you're older, that's what you'll be.
You'll have wings to fly and eyes to see,
That you can be whatever you dreamed,
And soon that is all what it seems.

Poppy Drew (9)
Great Bedwyn CE Primary School, Great Bedwyn

Death Woods

D eath Woods was a deep, dark and eerie place
E vil lurked all around.
A giant, foul beast rose from the swamps,
T he stench of the beast was repulsive.
H ow will we escape this beast?

W here could we hide and not be found?
O h, the silence of the woods.
O h, the darkness!
D are we move, dare we not?
S afety comes when I open my eyes, and realise it's all a dream.

Eddie Yorke (9)

Great Bedwyn CE Primary School, Great Bedwyn

The Nasty Teacher

"You smelly pig, you dirty rat!"
Said the teacher
With the pointy hat

"I don't like little squealers,
I'll run you down
With my four-wheeler."

The little child was meek and mild
What the teacher said
Made him wild

He hatched a plan, the little man
And put the teacher
In a pan

He added salt, he added chilli
And served her up
To his best mate Billy!

Max WIlsey (9)
Great Bedwyn CE Primary School, Great Bedwyn

Sweets Galore

I have just made this entirely edible cottage of sweets,
With lots and lots of my favourite treats.
It lurks in the middle of a beautiful forest with moss.
I am climbing up a mini tree whilst feasting on
candyfloss.
The outside of the house is made of delicious
gingerbread,
And upstairs Mentos for decorations on a bed.
The piano keys taste like sherbet and sunshine,
Now I'm full of sugar, I'm feeling fine!

Jessica Green (8)
Great Bedwyn CE Primary School, Great Bedwyn

Monkey Dee

As I close my eyes,
I enter a colourful fantastic world,
The soft sand and sea swirled,
I try to run but where are my feet?
Soaring through the skies in the heat,
A monkey flies next to me,
His name is Monkey Dee,
We play tag in the palm trees,
Having fun in the cool breeze,
Suddenly my alarm clock rings,
As I wake up and go on the swings,
I daydream about my friend Monkey Dee...

Harper Griffin (8)
Great Bedwyn CE Primary School, Great Bedwyn

Football Fantasy

The pitch is all ready, and to it I run,
As I look back cheerfully at people having fun,
No one can stop me, no matter how hard they try,
If we won the World Cup I'd feel such a high,
As the crowd becomes wild, I shoot, I score!
Then they let out a tremendous roar,
But then I wake up and hear my mother calling,
"Son, it's breakfast, and please stop snoring,"
Oh how boring.

Oliver Mendus-Edwards (8)
Great Bedwyn CE Primary School, Great Bedwyn

Dinosaurs

In my dreams every night
One of my dreams shines so bright
A land of magical dinosaurs
Leading me and my friends
To a castle, full of dens
The fairies trapped inside, their wings clipped
So they can't take to the sky
Don't worry, have no fear
The superheroes will soon appear
Lifted up by a superhero
A wizard spell and up they rose.

Jess Leslie (9)
Great Bedwyn CE Primary School, Great Bedwyn

Shimmering, Sparkling Fairy

F luttering, shimmering wings sparkle in the light
A little fairy out of sight
I don't believe my eyes saw right
R eally? Did that fairy just take flight?
I just saw a flash of white
E xcitement bubbled all around as I was full of delight
S ilently, the sun starts to set as it gradually turns to night.

Sophie Brown (8)
Great Bedwyn CE Primary School, Great Bedwyn

The Journey To The Beach

I once had an ant that I rode,
He lived next door to a toad,
There was a bird nearby,
Who had eaten a pie,
And took us to the beach by boat!
He flew out to sea,
To talk to a bee,
And suddenly realised we could float!
We rolled on our backs,
Saw a spacecraft beam,
And I woke up,
With a jolt from my dream!

Max Culmer (8)
Great Bedwyn CE Primary School, Great Bedwyn

Diving Kingfishers

In my dreams every night,
Diving kingfishers glide into the water with a beautiful
sight.
Wonderful wings and brilliant beaks,
They plummet into the water, is it fish they seek?

In the lovely sunny sky,
They elegantly fly.
Then the magic begins,
They start flying around and stars are coming out of
their wings!

Jake Levin (8)
Great Bedwyn CE Primary School, Great Bedwyn

Famous

In my dream I play basketball
Bouncing around the sports hall
With the crowd we're loud
Screaming with excitement.
When I slamdunk, the crowd is proud
Roaring with excitement
And I turn into a pro
Going low with the flow.
When I have the basketball I slamdunk
And the crowd is roaring with laughter.

Charlie Crees (9)
Great Bedwyn CE Primary School, Great Bedwyn

Friends

One day I went to play,
I saw a dancer and her name was Prancer.
She taught me some moves and grooves,
Then she challenged me but I always lose.
We lay on the floor and looked at the clouds and I was
really proud.

Tally
Great Bedwyn CE Primary School, Great Bedwyn

A Nightmare

As my eyes start closing, I see a new world unfolding,
Dead autumn leaves stretched across the ground,
I wonder in fear as I try not to make a sound,
Tall grim trees, shadows lurking by,
I quicken my pace as I try to hide my eyes.
Eerie whispers are now trapped inside my head,
I'm now longing to be back in my bed.
Thousands of glowing eyes following me around,
The wicked wind keeps pushing me about.

I begin to hear howls and owls and many other sounds,
They're all coming for me, I need to run *now!*
I speed away, I run for my life,
But what's that in the distance? Whatever it is, it's
definitely not nice!
It's racing towards me, I can now make out,
It's a humongous hungry bear!
It pounces with its huge mouth open,
Going through the air, and...

I wake up and gasp for air,
My heart beating so fast it might come out my chest.
"Thank goodness," I sigh with relief,
An autumn leaf then flies out the window and onto my
sheet.

Chichebem Biachi (11)
Holy Cross Catholic Primary School, South Ockendon

Once Upon A Dreamland

Once upon a delightful dream where the soothing
lullabies lead me,
Every fellow dances hand in hand while the music flows
so smoothly.
Once upon a swashbuckling dream in a dreadful pirate
land,
Cross those fingers or shall walk the plank and have
hoped you're on the island sand.
Once upon an adventurous dream, exploring with my
friends,
Fairies, pixies, where anything can happen, the fun can
never end,
I bet there isn't a better dream than being with all your
friends.
Once upon a teary dream, a princess has to part,
Locked away by her favourite prince, loves with all her
soul and heart,
Until she was banished to an abandoned land,
A dreadful life she had to start.
Once upon a happy saying who all have used to say,
Every heart may have a dream, an achievement they
have to start.
Whether good or better, aim with all your heart.

Dromoh Hammond (9)
Holy Cross Catholic Primary School, South Ockendon

That Mystical Star

In the dark winter city
Millions of stars brightened up across the sky
Children sleeping in their warm and comfortable beds
And that is when we all heard about that mystical star
Up deep in the galaxy there were stars
Lots and lots of them
But there was a star
Not a normal star, it was blue.
This star wasn't strong.
It wasn't courageous.
It wasn't amazing like all the others
They called it the powerless star.
This star was very lonely
And got bullied all the time
Powerless star was heading home.
Just a normal day
Sad and gloomy as usual.

Cianne Osei (10)
Holy Cross Catholic Primary School, South Ockendon

Fairies And Flies In Night Skies

Fairies shine so bright, everyone dancing in the light.
Fairies out night and day, horses asleep on the hay.
They fly above us in the clouds, just like a dove does all around.
I'm glad fairies came to this world, to add glory to others all around.
Fairies flying on their backs, to people planning an attack.
Fairies flying to their world, to dancers who had twirled and whirled.
Fairies flying higher and higher, so high they can touch the sky.
For now they just disappear, but we shall wait until perhaps next year.

Ella McNaughton (9)
Holy Cross Catholic Primary School, South Ockendon

Untitled

In the gleaming, morning sun,
The sun is shining and the flowers bloom.
The air is summer
And the fairies glow in the light of day.

A fairy comes and fairies go,
A crystal fairy accompanies me.
But let's see what treasures are there to find.
A rainbow comes into the gleaming light,
It shines so bright that my eyes are blind.

I wake up from my dream.
I wish I could go back to sleep!
But next time I dream,
I will have a better dream.

Eliana Atanda (9)
Holy Cross Catholic Primary School, South Ockendon

Once Upon A Dream

Once upon a dream where cows had wings,
Planets swirled around them,
All sorts of unusual things,
The cows were wild, with pink sparkles and gold,
The herd of cattle danced and pranced,
Their bright beautiful wings flapping,
Such a story to be told,
No grass or fields, just fluffy clouds and rainbows,
No mooing or milking,
Just angelic songs and strawberry Haribos,
When I awoke I heard my mum shout,
No more dreaming for me,
Someone let the cows out!

Elsabeth Yeates (9)
Holy Cross Catholic Primary School, South Ockendon

What I Do In Football

In my defence, I saved the ball.
Looking around the fence I tried to find the goal.
The passion, the motivation to dribble the ball.
Here I am in the middle of the field celebrating as I
score in front of you all.
I move the ball, I tackle the ball, I kick the ball.
Until they give up football.

Even when the game seems tough,
Against my opponents, my self-confidence drives me to
be a winner
But I couldn't be that if I wasn't a beginner.

Akintoyese Akinnunmé (8)
Holy Cross Catholic Primary School, South Ockendon

Dreamers

D ream dust helps people to have an imaginative and restful sleep,

R ising above the clouds to wondrous places,

E ach night, hoping that dreams come true.

A bove and beyond the twinkling stars the...

M agic flows!

E nter into your fantasy to make it your reality,

R each for your goals and

S weetly, silently dream...

Ruby Moore (8)
Holy Cross Catholic Primary School, South Ockendon

The Spy Who Killed Me

A fly went in my eye
So, I decided to buy myself a pie
They forgot the chicken thigh
I met a guy; I was a bit shy
But still said hi
The guy was actually a spy
He put poison in my pie
And I spilt my chai
I came back but when I took a bite
I was about to die
Until the spy said bye.

Rayn Zivarattinam (10)
Holy Cross Catholic Primary School, South Ockendon

Fortnite Is In Us

Fortnite grows
We kill and we try hard
We call people bots
And we explore new
Seasons grow, skins flow
While OGs take over the sweats
With lots left to show
Fortnite is fun
So it is to destroy
People fight till they die
While a wild community grows.

Alexander Valencia Ferreira (10)
Holy Cross Catholic Primary School, South Ockendon

Dragon

D aring as it walks towards me,
R oaring as the ground beneath me shakes,
A ll emotions running through my head,
G rowling at me with its fiery breath,
O nly me around to save myself,
N ot brave enough to open my eyes and face him.

Samuel Kinuthia Mburu (8)
Holy Cross Catholic Primary School, South Ockendon

Rain On Flowers In Autumn

As the rain falls on the flowers
Hour by hour
Little plants grow and flower
The rain so cold
And flowers so old
As the time flies by
The rain goes on flowers dry
Flowers blossom
Leaves awesome.

Melissa Valencia Ferreira (10)
Holy Cross Catholic Primary School, South Ockendon

Sleep

I sleep after seven hours and meet Pokémon in my
dream,
Then a blue book of poems takes all the Pokémon,
I am lonely, then I wake up to Pokémon.

Otitodilichukwu Jibunoh (9)
Holy Cross Catholic Primary School, South Ockendon

The Magical Bike

T o begin with, I was cycling into a forest to test a new bike.

H ow surprised was I when I found out it was magical?

E very time I thought of something it happened.

M ore things I thought about came true.

A fter more cycling, I just thought of going home and I got teleported.

G oing straight to my bed!

I woke again and went on my bike and I forgot it was a magical bike.

C an you actually believe that I forgot it was a magic bike?

A mazingly, I thought of something and it came true again!

L iverpool started playing against Man United right in front of me!

B rilliant game, Manchester won!

I mmediately I was on my bike again

K eeping the magic going while I ride my bike

E very time I ride my bike I make magic fun.

Cole Smith (11)
Kirkhill Primary School, Kincorth

New York Chaos

C heap food was running at me, so I put him down,
"H elp me!" I said, and then a plum that had spider legs was
A t the centre of New York, a pig fighting a dragon,
O h my god, an iron butt falling on the ground,
S o a random dwarf went in the crack and went to space.

W alking to a store and found a creepy man, so I went
I nvisible, chicken nuggets stealing money from people,
L enping RPG was shooting at things, and they went with a bang,
D anyry was coming like left and sandbag.

W alter came trying to sell the state to me; I ran,
I was scared for my life, so I hid, but a banana came over,
D ragging me to the battle and leaving, so I just stood there,
"E nd this now!" Turning but it got weird.

C areless eggs killing everyone around them,
R acing walking shoes racing around the city.
A ngry bouncy balls bouncing everywhere,
Z ig-zagging Amazon boxes zig-zagging,
Y ou'll love chine chony.

Michael Ziedins (12)

Kirkhill Primary School, Kincorth

The Red Guy

T he red guy: furry, big and trying to dig.
H e tried to get out but we tried to shout.
E ven his eye is bigger than a mini pie.

R oaming around a dark room with nothing but a broom
"E yes bigger than mini pies, that's cool," Kristers said.
D inner before bed was in my head. I wanted cake!

M y day has gone the other way, I can't today.
O nly I was the one to cry, "Oh why, why, why?"
N ear the wall trying to call but no hope at all.
S o close to the door that doesn't even open anymore.
T ired with nothing at all not even a ball.
E ven a key is good for me.
R ight now below me was a yellow key, we are free!

Jai McGowan (11)
Kirkhill Primary School, Kincorth

The Magical World

T utti frutti stars in a strange world,
H oney river flowing through the field,
E lderberries flying through the sky.

M ega chocolate in the shape of flowers,
A pples, cherries and strawberries are red,
G reen grass and lollipops all over the place,
I ce cream melting in your hands,
C andy Cane Lane, where everyone goes,
A cherry red in your eyes like candy canes,
L emonade in your mouth tastes good.

W atermelon shaped into pretty little stars,
O ranges are a fantastic food,
R aspberries are red, like a red dress,
L ime is a special taste like a lemon,
D ragon fruit is a nice fruit.

Kiara Haviarova (11)
Kirkhill Primary School, Kincorth

The Human Monster

I saw myself in a hall as big as a bus,
And as dark as black paint,
I went into the bus-sized hall where I saw a dinosaur,
Which was as fast as the world's fastest car.
I started to run like a deer,
But the dinosaur was so hungry and it looked like an old man,
The dinosaur caught me with his sticky fish hands,
Then it turned choppy as a slow computer,
I escaped the dinosaur,
But the hall ended with a wall, covered in honey,
It was as sticky as super glue,
The dino got me again with his breath,
That smelled like a million dead fish.
I woke up like I had one second to get ready for work,
Then I jumped like a rabbit and ran like Usain Bolt.

Oliver Ziedins (12)
Kirkhill Primary School, Kincorth

Pirate's Dream

P ost my mail to the postman

I need him to have it *now*!

R ight to the ship now!

A ndrew, hurry up! Terry, your teddy's here

T o the Caribbean we go, my fellow pirates!

E normous shark ahead, watch out!

D ive off, Mario and Kirby, go, go, go!

R ight, Brandon, you up there! Andrew, stay with me!

E veryone else get in your own position! Everyone, huge tentacles coming up! Come on, it's almost dead!

A mazing team, well done! It's defeated!

M arvellous the treasure we're heading for! But I woke up and turned on the TV and saw my dream had come true!

Harley Sutherland (11)
Kirkhill Primary School, Kincorth

Getting Lost

G ruesome noises were all around me and I was going crazy.

E erie objects that had faces also looked hairy.

T errifying bugs crawling on my legs.

T edious foxes that smell like eggs.

I tchy back is killing me, or is it the bugs that creep?

N ever have I ever been in the forest. It is as scary as it seems.

G lowing lights appeared in the sky.

L uminous snow falling sky-high

O dd creatures appearing from nowhere

S ome were wolves, rats and a bear

T urtles were flying and frogs couldn't jump, deer were running over speed bumps.

Tyler Wallace (11)
Kirkhill Primary School, Kincorth

Door To Door

Some nights, doors and doors fill
My head up with fright and delight.

In my dreams, door to door, I go
Some scary, some nice.

Monsters and mummies, fairies that fly.

I get further the more and more I go.

Most places are nice where bunnies roam.

But some are scary places I roam
I get lost in a river, hopefully I don't drift too far.

I wake up and the place I was drifting off to was all in my head!

Laci Forsyth (11)
Kirkhill Primary School, Kincorth

Wild Marvel Dreams

Iron Man swimming in the deep blue ocean
He was angry and felt emotion.

Thor's hammer flying through the sky
Attracting all the lightning and hitting every guy.

Spider-Man climbing up the high caverns
He shot his webs to control Thor's hammer.

Hulk in his form as loud as can be
He was sneaking around and couldn't be seen.

Mason MacDonald (11)
Kirkhill Primary School, Kincorth

Singer

S inging,
I ncredible,
N ervous,
G lamorous looking,
E xcited to sing,
R ainbow clothing.

O n stage,
N ew clothing!

S how-stopping performances,
T eamwork for the show,
A mazing singing,
G reat audience,
E xcellent food and drinks.

Ava Slatter (11)
Kirkhill Primary School, Kincorth

Funky Dreams

Once upon a time in a mystical landscape
There was a time when no one tried to escape
This land is happy but never ever sad
Here, everyone got along because no one was mad
In a church, there was a special hall
It was very special because it was tall
Outside the church was a magnificent house
It was even too big for a substantial mouse
This was a place where dreams can come true
A place where dreams are much bigger than you
This place was getting scary, I had no one to trust
Get out of this place I said I must
I rubbed my eye and scratched my head
And finally woke up to find I was in bed
For a second, I thought I might scream
But this I said was a funky dream.

Seth Hendry (9)
Lister Junior School, Tuebrook

It's All About Football

Every night I dream about winning the World Cup.
In my bright red shirt and my beautiful shiny boots
I walk onto the noisy pitch.
I hear the crowd roar.
All I want to do is score.
The most packed stadium I've seen,
Full of loud, happy, cheering fans.
You can hear them for miles and miles.
The game is all tied up.
One-all, this is serious.
There's only a couple of minutes left.
The keepers look super nervous as the team gets closer.
"Heads up," I hear. The ball comes near.
I take a touch then I shoot and I score!
Me and my team go crazy.
The fans are so happy and finally my dream has come true.

Harry Murney (10)
Lister Junior School, Tuebrook

Nature's Poem

The wind rustles the leaves of the tremendous trees;
As the flowers get pollinated by the beautiful bees;
The white fluffy clouds make nothing but a sound;
Whilst the birds chirp and fly all around;
Listen for the birds' song;
It's beautiful and lovely.

Be careful of the nests;
It's where the birds rest;
Trees are very tall and strong;
And their branches are very long;
The squirrels that like to eat nuts;
Use trees for their houses and huts;
Don't forget about trees; we really need to grow 'em;
This is nature's poem.

Nathan Kidd (10)
Lister Junior School, Tuebrook

To Become An Artist

My dream is to be an artist
Sometimes I wonder
What if my dream comes true?
My life will change
What if my dreaming becomes reality?
I also know how to make sculptures
I will sculpt humans
I will shade with pencils, paintings with acrylic paint,
Oil paint, pastel paint, watercolours
Fabric paint, oil pastels, crayons, sketch and painting brush
I found my happiness in painting, drawing
And sculpting on clay
I love them more than the sky.

Joanna Tom (9)
Lister Junior School, Tuebrook

The Sounds Of Mother Nature

Have you ever just sat down to listen to Mother
Nature's sounds?
It could be the swaying of the trees,
The stomping of an elephant, the crashing of the seas.
It could be a dog, a fish or a deer,
They're all sounds that we can hear.

Eva Barnes (9)
Lister Junior School, Tuebrook

Fluff The Cat

The morning rose for the cat
The cat ran for the hat
Once in shade, he scratched the small grey toy that
once was black
In sunlight, he stayed purring in the hat's shade
Fluff is his name
And loving food is his game.

Scarlett Rutland (10)
Lister Junior School, Tuebrook

Dragon

I had a dream and in that dream, I was a beautiful blue dragon.
I swished and swayed and wowed the crowd,
As I flew beyond my dreams.
I landed on a beautiful patch of flowers,
Not daydreaming for more hours.

Amelia Sarki (10)
Lister Junior School, Tuebrook

The Snow Globe

Here I lie in my cosy bed,
What a wonderful dream I have in my head,
The pearly white snow falls in my garden,
I wonder to this day why it doesn't harden,
How I walk into the kitchen gladly,
The smell of warm, fresh bread makes me feel so
dandy.

Oh, how I sometimes feel so lonely,
But I do not fear, my friend is near, oh how I like him so
knowingly,
When I walk outside I see the golden sun,
Oh, what a beauty nature has done,
I look up in the clear blue sky,
In a world where the birds don't fly.

I see a big friendly giant,
I stand not scared, I am resilient,
For I look him in the eyes,
He is just my friend, he has no evil lies,
As he knows I'm just a little girl in a little snow globe.

Nicole Golebiewska (11)
Little Parndon Primary Academy, Harlow

Mars

I'm on Mars,
A planet of stars,
It's so big,
But it's wearing a wig,
For what we don't know,
Is hiding below,
There are aliens plotting,
And monsters dotting,
They are far away,
But we start to sway,
Everything spins,
And you land in a bin,
When you wake,
You give a little shake,
And standing next to you is Bob,
But he's not here to rob!
He is scary!
But somehow sweet, like a fairy!
He shows you around,
And you start to bound,
And bounce,
And boing,
But you're sad to see,

It's only glee,
The shaking is real,
Because your mum's made a meal!
For you've seen plenty of red,
You're safe in bed!

Laura Macovei (11)
Little Parndon Primary Academy, Harlow

Save Our Planet

S afely in my dreams, in my head

A s I wonder, "Am I safe once I am outside of bed?"

V ery easy to answer, "No"

E ither it's crime or global warming, which is bigger you should know

O ur planet is beautiful

U nited we can make it wonderful

R ebuilding our planet, we all need to help

P lease help to replenish our kelp

L oving our ocean is one of the best things we can do

A s well as not using fossil fuels, which helps too

N ot nearly enough are helping to pitch in

E ither we help or this will become our sin

T hank you for reading my poem.

Toby Wilsher (10)
Little Parndon Primary Academy, Harlow

Spider Royalty

Spiders are royalty
Royalty is radical
Me and Rosie skipped through the dark forest
Me and Rosie were alarmed when we saw Spider
Royalty
A big colossal spider
Me and Rosie were petrified
We hated spiders
But we know we should not be afraid of them
But this one was huge
We were curious so we went up to it
It said hi
We were scared so we ran back.

Tegan Knowles (10)
Little Parndon Primary Academy, Harlow

Royalty

To be royalty, you need loyalty.
You need a gown but no frown.
You need a crown with a bow.
You need a story but not glory.
You need a wand but not a bond.
You need to be polite, but not twice.
You need to write but don't be right.
You need a pet that won't get you wet.

This is royalty, hopefully with loyalty.

Paris Gibson (11)
Little Parndon Primary Academy, Harlow

Spiders

S ecret spiders creep and crawl,
P assing time like no other as they duel
I n the corners of your room you will meet
D iscarded creatures who weep
E choing screams as they crawl toward you
R iding on webs as a few
S ecret spiders creep and crawl.

Emilie Sims (10)
Little Parndon Primary Academy, Harlow

As Sweet As Sugar Can Be

As sweet as sugar can be,
Too much is not good for me!

Sugar in sweets, sugar in drinks and much much more.
Things without sugar can be such a bore.

Sugar is light,
Sugar is bright,
But never eat sugar in the night!

Zoha Awan (10)
Little Parndon Primary Academy, Harlow

Love Someone

It doesn't matter what you put on,
I will still love you to the moon and back,
You are my everything,
You are what everyone wants,
You're loyal, kind, smart, pretty, loving and sweet,
So can I be your everything?

Harry Cockman (11)
Little Parndon Primary Academy, Harlow

Magic

In the land of magic
Where the unicorns gallop
Where stars lie in the sky
And the fireflies fly
Where the wishes come true
And the dragons flew
Where the dreamers dream
And the singers sing.

Evie Mary-Jean Yeo (11)
Little Parndon Primary Academy, Harlow

Feathers

Feathers fall from the sky
Reminding us that an angel is nearby
Angel wings wrap around us
Showing that their love has never left us.

James Patten (10)
Little Parndon Primary Academy, Harlow

Lost In The Forest

In my dreams, I am taken to a deep dark forest
I walk by and start exploring all its attractive aspects,

I look up at the azure-rich sky full of stars,
But all so suddenly, I leap in fear, to see a black jaguar.
But feel comfortable to see an elephant with calm demure,
Shaking its mighty, enormous head in friendly cheer!

I continue to explore further,
But then I hear *her*...
'The Lioness Queen'
Standing proudly in the green.

I am taken aback by her mighty presence,
And shaken with her sheer elegance!
The lioness is calm, quiet alongside her cub,
I make my way back to my sleepy hub...

To end my poem, I shall say,
The beauty of the forest looks mesmerising all through the day
Let's save our forest and our animals,
And then only our planet can be magical.

Adrija Das Gupta (10)
Mendell Primary School, Bromborough

88

Dreams...

Daddy gives a hug,
Mummy gives a kiss,
I then listen for the door to slam closed,
I soon realise I'm in my dreams!
What wonders will I see?
A unicorn as bright as the sun
But filled with a rainbow, oh what fun!
A glowing dragon with her wings
Twirls along, oh how cool, so much fun!
Soon I see a flying horse with a starlit tail
And purple galaxy mane
What a wonder to see today,
Later on, I find I'm in bed
At home, snug like a little sausage roll
Can't wait for tomorrow's dreams to arrive.

Amber-Rose Philpott (10)
Mendell Primary School, Bromborough

Starstruck

Perfectly normal day,
Just like the rest,
Rush to school, friends waiting
Exactly the same all the time.
Suddenly, in walks Taylor Swift,
Looks around, walks over and sits down next to me.
"Why are you here?" I ask her,
"I go to school here," she tells me, "like you."
I'm shocked, confused,
Excitement floods my brain.
Taylor Swift is sitting next to me!
I'm awestruck. I'm floored,
Such an honour to meet Taylor Swift.

Emma Scott (10)
Mendell Primary School, Bromborough

Darkness

When I sleep tight in my little bed
The little things that happen in my tiny head
Are things you do *not* want to know.
Like all the creepy animals such as a crow.
The darkness surrounds me like a pack of geese
As the monsters come - ugh, they give me the creeps!
The things that scare me will surely make you pee!
There is nothing more that I am scared of other than
the darkness.
Just remember this is all in my room
Where there is nothing but gloom.

Archie Williams (9)
Mendell Primary School, Bromborough

The Broadcaster

Here comes the broadcaster, the narrator talks,
The man who can see but no eyes at all,
Here comes the broadcaster, as still as a stone,
His head is electronics, even a phone,
He moves through the night, dark and alone.
Hello, broadcaster, how do you see?
I mean, your head is a literal TV.
He comes when nothing can turn on,
When all the city's lights are magically gone.
Here comes the broadcaster,
The man who can see, but no eyes at all.

George Lloyd (9)
Mendell Primary School, Bromborough

A School Nightmare

I am ready to fly to school,
I am nervous, this is why...

S is for sensitive
C is for crying
H is for horror
O is for overwhelming
O is for overthinking
L is for learning.

Grace Lavinia Gladwin (10)
Mendell Primary School, Bromborough

My Dreams

D is for danger
R is for real
E is for experience
A is for adventure
M is for mischievous
S is for scared.

Emily Henshaw (9)
Mendell Primary School, Bromborough

If I Went To Sleep, I Would Dream...

If I went to sleep, I would dream of...

Dazzling fairies twirling around and magical horses flying amongst the clouds,

With majestic unicorns strutting around, their moonlit hair falling gracefully to the ground,

And flowers planted elegantly, all big or small,
Every flower would be unique, no flower the same at all,

The stars would twinkle and gleam against the royal blue blanket in the sky,
And the owl's hoots would echo endlessly throughout the silent night.

Suddenly I could feel a supernatural mist linger near
As I watched the universe disappear.

"Bye-bye!" I said, "I'll see you soon!"
And I woke up to the sounds of snoring from the other bedroom.

Sarah Tekle (11)
Pilgrim Primary Academy, Plymouth

Dream

Dream
What is a dream?
A place full of rainbows and tea parties
Or is it a place of nothing?
Is it a dream that can be fulfilled
Or a dream that will fill you with grief?
They say dream big
What happens when it cannot be fulfilled?
Or maybe a dream is a place to escape the real world.
You may want to be rich or famous
And that can be done... sometimes.
A dream could be full of potions and pastries that can make you grow tall
Like forests and cottages.
Kids, if you're reading this, don't give up on your dreams like I did.
Keep going and who knows, you might get a happy ·
ending... or not.
Not every story has a happy ending.

Alison Oldfield (11)
Pilgrim Primary Academy, Plymouth

Fairy Land

Here come me and my little sister,
We started to play Twister.
Then we saw a little door,
So we turned into a cat and scratched it with a claw.
We went inside and saw a beach,
Some fairies came up and said a little speech.
"The king and queen want to see you,"
So we followed the little crew.
"Welcome to the royal ball,
We have our own pool.
Please join the ball,
You can swim in our pool.
Just go and dance,
We know how to prance.
Don't be shy."
"We need to cry.
This seems kind of sketchy,
And is kind of messy.
Let's prance out of here.
Let's go somewhere near."

Sienna Newton (9)
Pilgrim Primary Academy, Plymouth

I Had A Dream...

I had a dream, it made me beam
I had a dream that I could fly as high as a butterfly
I had a dream that I was floating on cloud nine
I had a dream that I felt like a kid given a dime
I had a dream of being in front of a line that was as long as a lifetime
I had a dream that I danced under the rain while it quenched the thirst of this earth
I had a dream
I had a dream
I had a dream
I had a dream but a dream is just a dream, never reality
At least that's what they say
It's as sweet as honey
Or as nice as a summer's day
For others, dreams are just a causality
But for me, it's an abnormality.

Joyce Lopes (10)
Pilgrim Primary Academy, Plymouth

Night Watcher

Heavy eyelids open,
Only to be relieved by billions of beaming stars,
Upon a dark cobalt sky.
As they surround me,
From every view, the eye can see,
I slowly look down, unaware of what is supporting me.
Underneath my hand is a soft, milk cloud,
I notice the loud vivid lights of the city,
Up ahead I notice a fairy,
She's wearing a gorgeous golden and black robe,
Her skin is pale white, like the moon,
She has long black locks that wave and glimmer in the moonlight,
I smile and realise she's the night watcher.

Edlyn Hayfron-Taylor (11)
Pilgrim Primary Academy, Plymouth

Night Dreams

I had a dream
About a scheme
With my team
I went to a shop
While listening to bebop
But the door was locked
Me and my team
Were eating cheese
When we were finished
When we were done
My team had a number one
While in the shop
We were happy, then we saw a tally
I wondered what it was
Then a cat came with its paws
We screamed and ran
And got hit by a pan
I woke up mad
And then I turned mad
My sister hit me with a golf club.

Arsema Muluebirhan (11)
Pilgrim Primary Academy, Plymouth

The Invisible Man

Where am I?
Where is me?
I'm invisible,
That is all I can see.
I'm holding a suitcase,
And I see a face,
Is that me?
I'm wearing a coat,
A coloured green coat,
I have thick black shoes,
That I could never lose.
I feel so sad,
A splash of mad,
And I don't know why,
It's not divine.
I'm invisible,
Yet my emotions are divisible,
Well, today I've learned,
I'm invisible.

Lacey Williams (10)
Pilgrim Primary Academy, Plymouth

The Sweet, Sweet Sky

The sweet sweet sky looks
So so sweet, the so sweet sky feels
So so fluffy with its so pink
Clouds in the pinkish-purple sky
With the white quarter moon
Oh the sky so sweet
The so fluffy unicorns
Dancing on so colourful rainbows
In the sky that is oh so sweet
The sky that is oh so sweet
Thinks that it's time to sleep
As the unicorns start to sleep
The half moon turns full
See you tomorrow, sweet sweet sky.

Lola-Rose Wilson (10)
Pilgrim Primary Academy, Plymouth

My Dreams...

I dream of shooting stars,
I dream of chocolate bars,
I dream of magic wands,
I dream of endless ponds,
I dream of daring dragons who fly high through the night,
I dream of pirates who steal and fight,
I dream of magic beans,
And they do make a scene!
I dream of riding cars,
I dream of being a movie star!
I dream of flying high,
And see chickens flying by!
I dream of sushi rolls,
I dream of bowling balls!

Marcus Wang (11)
Pilgrim Primary Academy, Plymouth

Welcome To The Hotel

I stand up to see,
A hotel in front of me.
I find one or two,
Who can build Lego without you.
I book a room,
Which may be in doom.
I get into the elevator,
Which has a lot of buttons.
Suddenly, I get stuck,
Which gives me no luck.
I hear an eerie sound,
Coming out of a mouth.
A doll starts running,
I close my eyes since my brain is not cunning.
Soon, I wake up to see,
It's just a dream...

Jan Grzybowski (11)
Pilgrim Primary Academy, Plymouth

Dreams

Your dreams can be big
And small,
You've got to choose
But you can't have them all.

It can be sword fighting
It can be dragons clashing,
But only choose one
Or else you will be a silly pun
With one bun!

So just remember,
You've got to choose
But you can't have them all.

It can be a mythical creature
It can be a famous footballer,
So choose one.

Sophia Jobbins (11)
Pilgrim Primary Academy, Plymouth

The Moon And Stars

I dream of seeing the moon as bright as the sun
It makes me shine like the morning star
Over the hill and far away
Waiting for the moon and the star to rise
On the beautiful night
You can see the stars and the moon
And wait for them to rise again
It makes me glimmer
When it rises.

Gabrella Oshilim (8)
Pilgrim Primary Academy, Plymouth

Dreams

D reams, dreams, we all dream,

R eal ones and fake ones,

E asy ones, hard ones and some in-between,

A gain and again,

M y mind plays games on me, I try to ignore it, but I can't,

S ad ones, happy ones, they all try to wake me up, but they can't.

Hollie Goff (10)
Pilgrim Primary Academy, Plymouth

Scarlett And The Horse Land

In my dream every night,
Fairies fly very bright,
Horses running in the lane,
People waving from the train,
One by one the carriages passed,
The horses galloped, the fairies flew fast,
Everyone looked at the sunset,
It's a moment no one will forget.

Scarlett Bailey (8)
Pilgrim Primary Academy, Plymouth

I Like

I like pancakes,
I like sweets,
I like cake,
When I wake up.
I like basketball
When it rains.
I like sunshine,
I like sand,
I like brown leaves
When they blow.
I like collies,
I like cats,
I like clowns
In funny hats.

Alya Mohammed (9)
Pilgrim Primary Academy, Plymouth

Your Dreams

As you close your eyes in your dreams
You wake in a world full of joy
Gallop with unicorns or set sail on a ship
You can make anything come true in your dream
Dream big to think big
Dreaming is not limited
Dreaming is your choice of view.

Aisha Akanji (10)
Pilgrim Primary Academy, Plymouth

Dreaming

Royalty and unicorns
Monsters and fairies too
In the wonderful world of dreaming
They all gather for you.
The possibilities are endless
There's no need to be frightened
The world is your oyster
Everything is exciting.

Phoebe Hepburn-Phillips (11)
Pilgrim Primary Academy, Plymouth

Tom And The Socket

In my dream I have a gorilla called Tom,
And get all the clean socks and try to make the socket.
A rocket made out of socks.
We needed one more sock.
I saw a rainbow sock
It was more vibrant than the actual rainbow.
Tom was building the great socket
And the last sock came flying at Tom
Thankfully he caught it and it was complete.

Me and Tom bunched into the colourful masterpiece.
Tom grabbed the button and *smack!*
Then *boom!*
We flew away into the angelic stars.
Moments later we landed on the rings of Saturn
And Tom asked to race around the rings.
I said yes.
We laughed all through the race
But it was time to go home.
I jumped on the socket, so did Tom.
The socket quickly jet into space
And I woke up in my bed.

Frankie McGuire (10)
St Bartholomew's Primary School, Glasgow

The Pink Fluffy Dog

Last night, I had the weirdest dream.
It was about a pink dog.
It was as soft as clouds, and as pink as fresh cotton candy (yum yum)
And its eyes were as green as emeralds,
But that wasn't the weird thing.
It had wings and could talk!
Flying around the world
We landed in space.
It was *amazing*.
I could see Neptune, Venus, Jupiter, Uranus, Mercury, Saturn, Mars,
And don't forget Earth.
But then we saw aliens. I was terrified.
The aliens were a mixture of colours.
One was pistachio, two were turquoise, three were peach,
Four were salmon and five were bubblegum.
So, in total, there were fifteen aliens chasing us.
I wish I could dream about that again.

Quinn Brogan (9)
St Bartholomew's Primary School, Glasgow

Pink Fluffy Unicorns

P ink unicorns, pink as candy floss,
I n our hats are marshmallows,
N utritious sweets are our dreams,
K nowing we are the best.

F luffy unicorns like a sheep,
L ollipops for us to eat,
U nique as other creatures,
F luffy unicorns dancing on rainbows,
F lying through the sky,
Y oghurts are great for us.

U nicorns as pink as a raspberry,
N ot like a dragon can beat us,
I n our island, we dance all night,
C ute as a newborn baby,
O ur powers are magical,
R unning like a cheetah,
N one can beat us,
S queaky voices like car tyres.

Mollie French (10)
St Bartholomew's Primary School, Glasgow

Time Traveller

Making this machine was harder than I thought,
I couldn't even use the things I bought,
When suddenly *zap! Bang!* All my tools went flying,
"What just happened? Oh wow, I think this is a crime,"
My time machine, it's finally on,
I skipped and jumped and ran around and had a blast
but what I didn't know was...
An actual blast would happen and I would gasp!
When I got sucked into this colourful tunnel,
"Wow, where am I? Is that what I think it is? That's a
castle,"
Made out of sweets, there were so many candy canes,
I was so happy till I woke up, although it was a dream, I
still loved it.

Freya Molloy (10)
St Bartholomew's Primary School, Glasgow

Dragon Dreams

D ragons are nice, dragons are sweet.

R ight in my dream, I saw them asleep.

A sleep on the grass, they woke up with a roar.

G oing on through the path, I happened to see more.

O n the way, I saw unicorns grazing on hay.

N ight arose but everyone wanted me to stay.

D ark it was but the stars made me light.

R oars came from the sky which was so bright.

E lves appeared right in my front and took me in.

A ll of the elves let me stay except for an elf Tin.

M ighty ogres arose from the land.

"S tay," they said, but I had already ran.

Kamsiyochukwu Joshua Uzor (10)
St Bartholomew's Primary School, Glasgow

Flying Car

Bored of staying on the ground
I don't like looking around.
I wish my car could fly so high
It is my dream to fly in the sky.

I drove my car to the top of the roof
After a while a guard dog woofs!
I drove my car off the roof, almost crashing
But then a miracle happened and I was flying!

It was nice to be in the sky with the birds
I want to do fractions in the sky; my favourite fraction is a third.
I brought my PS5 with me in the car
I even ate my favourite chocolate bar.

I woke up from this dream
It was better than my favourite scented cream.

Iyanuoluwa Oni (10)
St Bartholomew's Primary School, Glasgow

Why Witches Stare

Bubble bubble toiling trouble, fire crawling double bubble,
Witches laugh to their cruel end, bubbles floating through the air,
Witches laughing like they just don't care,
Fire flames flickering through the air.
Thirty-seven demon eggs roaming through the air,
Something to say before you get scared,
If you ever met a witch better don't stare.
How could I have dreamt of this scary cruel dream?
Only in my nightmare on the day of Halloween.

Winifred Ubah (11)
St Bartholomew's Primary School, Glasgow

The Rat House

Every time I go to sleep,
I see something horrifying.
It's a house but it is abandoned
And crumbled and infested with rats!

I wake up inside the rat house,
In a room with only a bed and a chair.
I am in the bed, the floor is cheese,
And there are no walls.

I stand up and get dragged
To a shrine by the rats,
And they make me their god!

Stephen Ross (10)
St Bartholomew's Primary School, Glasgow

Broony Boy

Broony is my dog and he's brown, black and white.
Our dog is named after Scot Brown,
But the cool thing is we got Broony the night Scot Brown left.

Broony is two-and-a-half years old,
I wish Broony could drive me to school, I mean fly me to school,
That's my dream.

Broony is my favourite thing ever,
Obviously, my mum and dad are first!

Ella-Mae O'Brien (9)
St Bartholomew's Primary School, Glasgow

The Rat Room

Once upon a dream,
There's a room called the Rat Room.
It is a bedroom in the rat houses.
The bed smells like rat-flavoured cheese,
The floor is cheese.

Once you sleep,
You dream of a gigantic rat chasing you in a block of cheese!
Now when you get caught,
You will have cheese for toes when you sleep!

Zoey McLaren (10)
St Bartholomew's Primary School, Glasgow

Rat In The Woods

There was a rat on a hat,
There was also a bat and a cat,
The rat was on a flute,
The cat was on a chute!

The bat was on a bat,
On a mat, the cat sat.
The rat was with a rat,
The cat ate the bat and the rat...
...And that was that!

Braxton James (10)
St Bartholomew's Primary School, Glasgow

What Cockapoos Do In A Dream

First they go to the zoo that smells like poo,
Then run about fast like they are having a blast,
Then dance to tunes so they can play with the
balloons,
They like to bite with all their might,
I wonder what they dream at night?

Kacey McCallion (10)
St Bartholomew's Primary School, Glasgow

There Was A Rat In A Hat

There was a rat in a hat,
That had a suit with a flute.
In a chute in the woods with some wood.
The rat made a fire, but his pants were on fire!
Then he was as black as charcoal...
And learned not to play with fire.

Noah Sisawo (10)
St Bartholomew's Primary School, Glasgow

Forest Fairies

When I woke up from a very good sleep,
I saw a weird door, should I take a peep?
I got out of bed, and tiptoed to the door,
Okay, it was time to go in there. Time to explore.

As I went in, I took a few steps,
To see a forest as green as can be,
With beautiful blue skies,
What else can I see?

As I kept walking, I got more and more scared,
When something in front of me hovered and glared,
It was two or three fairies! Yes, this is true,
There were big ones, tall ones and little ones, too,
A bright cherry-red fairy came at me and said,
"Can you play with us?"
We played for more than half an hour
In a magical playground with a very tall tower.

I started to get sleepy, I needed to rest,
But suddenly I saw a big beam,
I woke up, it was all just a dream.

Layla Gorman (10)
St George's Primary School, Portland

Alice In Dragon Land

Once upon a time,
Not so long ago,
Lived a girl named Alice
Not the Alice from Wonderland though.
Her life was normal,
Her dream was to be a florist,
But her mum would not let her,
So she ran away to the forest.

Her life was simple there,
Alice all alone
This day whilst riding her horse,
The sky went black all of a sudden
Alice saw two big eyes staring,
Big emerald eyes.
Her face froze as water into ice,
Alice screamed aloud.
Although her face paralysed
With this new fear,
A grin appeared on this creature's face,
But not a horrid sneer,
Just a gentle smile,
That gave Alice no fear.

As Alice edged backwards,
She felt cold, bumpy scales,
The sun appeared through the leaves,
And lit a blue and purple tail,
Alice gasped, "And wings!"
"Dragon... Ahh!" she screamed.
And then touched the dragon's face,
Alice, with a smile, said,
"You look like a Violet."
The dragon shook her head.
"No? A... Scarlet,
I think, instead."

So Alice and Scarlet lived together,
By the way, it was to be forever...
Happily!

Grace Peters-Daw (9)
St George's Primary School, Portland

Lies

Flying on my broomstick, through the dark skies,
Thinking of all those boys who tell lies.
They need to be taught a lesson in truth,
Otherwise, they could end up losing a tooth.
Or growing a wart on the back of their tongue,
With breath smelling of dragon's dung.

Cauldrons and newts, beetles and bats,
Ground to a pulp to cause panic attacks.
Many a boy thinks they are so wise,
But still, they're telling stupid lies!
To teach them a lesson they need to be told,
If they don't stop, they will be sold.

The witch in the forest loves little boys,
She uses them for her little cats' toys,
The cats toss them about like bowling balls,
The boys start to cry out with manic calls.
No one can hear them screaming aloud,
Soon their bodies will be covered in a shroud.

Holly-Jean McAllister-Naylor (9)
St George's Primary School, Portland

Once Upon A Million Dreams

I dream to be a dancer and a boxer,
Doesn't that sound odd!
But if you have belief,
Your dreams can come true.
I've been preparing myself all my life
And now it's coming true.
I dream in the stars and dance with the moon.
I've been getting awards for my dreams,
So I know I'll go beyond.
I have nightmares me and my friend get split up,
And I don't know what's coming next!
Help me start to find my way back home.
Imagine this is me in a boxing ring,
Becoming a world champion.
Imagine this is me on a stage,
Dancing my heart out.
I'd be gazing at the stars,
Hoping for good news,
But it's not just the stars that make your dreams come true,
It's truly you!

Lillie Laing (9)
St George's Primary School, Portland

The Pirate Princess

The Pirate Princess sailed the seas,
Her ship was fast, her crew did please,
She wore a hat with a feather so grand,
And a sword at her side, always at hand.

Her hair was long, her eyes were bright,
She laughed and sang with all her might,
She searched for treasure, gold and jewels,
And never once did she act like a fool.

Her heart was brave, her spirit was free,
She was the best pirate at the sea,
Her name was known from shore to shore,
And all that met her did adore.

So if you see her ship on the waves,
Don't be afraid, don't be afraid,
Just wave hello, and shout her name,
And she'll be sure to do the same.

Willow-Rose Day (10)
St George's Primary School, Portland

Practice Makes Perfect

Practice makes perfect,
So when you're on stage,
All you have to do...
Is flip to the next page.

So don't do what I did
One awful night,
But even though it was a dream...
It's a dancer's worst sight.

I was on stage, doing my part,
Until I felt like someone shot my heart.
I had fallen to the floor!
I was on my hands and knees.

So obviously this isn't,
The best of happy ending,
Because all I was trying to do,
Was keep blending and blending and blending.

So the moral of the story,
Is to practise every day,
So it can feel like
You can just float away.

Skylar Conlan (10)
St George's Primary School, Portland

The Dream Dragon

In the mystical mountains, where the sun sets in the East,
Lives a mysterious creature, who some call a foul beast,
Twisting and twirling, it snakes through the air,
Retreating into its secret lair.

Unfortunately, the misunderstood creature stays in the shadows,
Safely hidden on the mountain plateau,
Shimmering scales, resembling a mermaid's tail,
Protecting the creature, and keeping it well.

Its eyes dazzle bright, reflecting the winter moonlight,
It sleeps in the day and comes out at night,
If you ever see it, it'll give you a fright!

Matilda Fairman (9)
St George's Primary School, Portland

Springtopia

When me and my friends had nothing to do,
We went to Springtopia
And nobody knew,
We sat on the shiny grass,
It felt nice to be relaxed and not in class!
We watched the floating clouds go by,
And it almost felt like we could fly,
Then we ate some food,
And it sounded quite funny when the cows mooed!
Put on your lip balm,
And you'll feel really calm,
Unfortunately, it was time to go,
But everyone was upset though,
Later that day I was comfy in bed,
With thoughts of Springtopia that stayed in my head.

Ella Ward (9)
St George's Primary School, Portland

Screams And Dreams

I close my eyes and soon I'm there,
In a place so cold and bare.
I enter a house full of negativity,
And fill it up with my positivity.
By shutting away the dark and turning on the light,
Something as simple as that made it all happy and bright.
I added a swing set and a slide,
I added some colour and a pony you can ride.
For it started so I'd shout and scream,
Turns out it was just a lovely dream.
Just like every dream it was all in my head,
And a few minutes later I woke up in bed.

Emily Woodcock (10)
St George's Primary School, Portland

My Adventurous Ambitions

I want to be an explorer,
I want to be a star,
I want to be an astronaut,
And be the first to step on Mars!

I want to be a footballer,
And score twenty goals in one match!
I want to be a gardener,
And grow a massive pumpkin patch!

I want to design costumes,
For every single play,
I want to write and illustrate books,
All day, every day.

I want to be a beautician,
I want to direct shows,
Or films or animations,
That everyone will know.

Imogen Burley (10)
St George's Primary School, Portland

The Golden Butterfly

I sat in the fall of fireflies,
What passes, a golden butterfly.
Its wings are fragile with solid ore,
I've never seen anything like it before!

What a sight, what a scene,
Under the dusk sun, it glows,
Flutter nearby, flutter me low,
Flutter me light, and flutter my soul.

Fly away, little one, wherever shall you go,
Go back home, you shall flow,
In the dusky, cold and dark night,
Let's hope you're still there, tomorrow night.

Isobel Comben (10)
St George's Primary School, Portland

Who Runs The World? Girls!

Zoom! went the ball down through the pitch,
Lauren James has done it, like Perfect Pitch,
Chloe Kelly plays matches just as well,
The other girl footballers are well fell.

Zoom! went the ball down through the pitch,
Lauren James has done it, like Perfect Pitch,
England came home from the Euros and won,
But the World Cup wasn't nicely done.

Next time we hope for the best,
Come on England, let's be next.

Isla Porter-Bargery (10)
St George's Primary School, Portland

My Dream Is Your Dream

Stars up high in my twinkling eyes,
My dreams are right in front of me,
How can I visualise?
All I know now, this is what it's meant to be.
High up in the sky, in my rocket,
Blasting through the air.
Now I have reached my target,
And no, it wasn't a dare,
This is true, this is real life!
I'm a girl, I'm proud, it's me!
Now let me enjoy my grand flight.
Remember be you, be free, be who you want to be.

Orla White (9)
St George's Primary School, Portland

Hollywood

I'm very famous,
My clothes are shameless,
I get to go to Hollywood,
And show my girlhood.

It is so awesome,
That I get to blossom,
I tried a show
They said I was a pro.

And now I star in more movies,
It is very roomy,
I get my own compartment
In an apartment.

So now I live in Hollywood,
My dream since childhood,
But oh no, it's morning,
I've had to wake up, warning!

Kiahola-Joan Coker (10)
St George's Primary School, Portland

Xander's Dream Of Becoming A YouTuber

I looked up, and I saw a camera filming me.
I started with a YouTube video about
How to look after a little brother but it was boring,
But I know to never give up.

So, I made another one.
One called 'How to make a mushroom farm',
But people just kept getting sick.
So, I made one more, and it was called,
'A brown mushroom farm',
And it was perfect.
I was really happy.

Xander Hibell (9)
St George's Primary School, Portland

Nightmares

N ightmares make you toss and turn,

I nside your heart and stomach churn,

G rinning clowns with blood on their face,

H owling reapers holding a mace.

T itanic sinking into the deep,

M ighty toads and frogs do leap,

A rmies stuck knee-deep in mud,

R un or you will shed your blood,

E nding when you wake,

S ilently you begin to quake.

Micah Lively (9)
St George's Primary School, Portland

Space Race

S oaring through the sky on my way to space
P lanets and stars in this wide-open place
A round I go with Earth below
C hasing Lewis Hamilton, here I go!
E veryone is watching from their TV screens.

R acing Hamilton is one of my dreams
A m I going to win the space race?
C heering and clapping here I come
E veryone watches, yes I won!

Charlie Matterface (10)
St George's Primary School, Portland

Trials

In my dreams, I ride my bike,
Sometimes I go with Mike,
We like to go up the hills,
We've had a few petrol spills.

We balance when we ride over rocks,
When we aren't riding, we use our locks.
Sometimes we take lunch,
That's if we haven't had brunch.

When it rains it tends to flood,
But they're the best times because we get covered in mud.

JJ Porter Cross (10)
St George's Primary School, Portland

In The Dark

In the dark it's nice and quiet,
No children outside causing a riot.

In the dark it's nice and warm,
Won't be long before a storm.

In the dark the wind will blow,
Waiting for tomorrow to say hello.

In the dark the sun will hide,
But shall be back full of pride.

In the dark I close my eyes,
To wake refreshed at sunrise.

Lois Westwood (10)
St George's Primary School, Portland

Dragons

D reading this night by far.

R evolting dragons creep through the door ajar.

A m I asleep, is this a dream?

G ot to keep my eyes open, I'm seeing this fiend,

O range eyes staring at me,

N obbly skin as red as can be.

S hall I run before it's too late, oh it's just my mum telling me it's 8!

Maisie Norris (9)
St George's Primary School, Portland

Circus Of Fun

C reepy crawly clowns
I s spraying each other
R ight in their faces.
C lashing together
U p and down,
S ide by side,

O n and all over each other.
F antastic flying monkeys

F orever flying high,
U nderneath the dogs
N earby the jumping frogs.

Ruby Hicks (9)
St George's Primary School, Portland

Tornado

T owering trees blowing fiercely in the breeze
O ften followed by terrifying screams,
R otating relentlessly
N obody is safe,
A yell from the distance, "It's coming my way."
D estroying and smashing everything in its path
O pened my eyes, I was asleep in the bath!

Noah Flavell (9)
St George's Primary School, Portland

My Dream

Safe and sound in my bed,
With leaping frogs going round my head.
Each one beginning to glow,
Every night I love the show.
In the end they have to say goodbye,
Waking me up with a sign,
Closing one eye and off I go again.
Here come the froggies with another act
Maybe 10.

Phoebe Wilson (10)
St George's Primary School, Portland

Sometimes I Dream

Sometimes I dream of flying sheep,
With fairy wings and chicken feet.
Sometimes I dream I am a teacher,
In ancient Rome with Julius Caeser.
Sometimes I dream of giant ducks,
Driving cars and racing trucks.
All my dreams come from my head,
When I'm sleeping in my bed.

Maddie Carney (10)
St George's Primary School, Portland

Foodland

All the food I see,
Is a heaven to me,
Lollipops as trees,
Milky chocolate bars,
The house is made of sweets,
Filled with toffee treats.
Dripping caramel in the clouds,
What's that popping sound?
Popping candy I see.
I'm as hungry as could be.

Jax Moore (9)
St George's Primary School, Portland

Holiday

H appy times away from home
O n a special journey
L ovely views out my bedroom window
I n my bed warm and snug
D og walks and adventures
A ltogether sat around the fire
Y ou would love it too!

Annabel Barnes (10)
St George's Primary School, Portland

A Dream I'm Yet To Open...

In a dream, I'm yet to open,
Dino pirates have awoken.

Dragons and krakens in the air,
Fighting the axolotl, very unfair.

In a dream, I'm yet to open,
Possibilities can never be broken...

Dominic Gault (9)
St George's Primary School, Portland

Singing With K-Pop

In my dream I can see people around me
On stage with Blackpink makes me feel and think
I'm getting famous, really happy and excited
Using the microphone to sing out loud
To people in the crowd.

Demi-Lola Roberts (9)
St George's Primary School, Portland

At The Flying Pigs Disco

In my dreams every night,
Flying pigs are in my sight,
Dancing far and dancing near,
Happy pigs are all I hear,
Shining lights, also bright,
Flying pig discos are such a delight!

Ruby Grant Jones (9)
St George's Primary School, Portland

Space Jump

S uper jump to the moon,

P ractice safety,

A ssure your location,

C rystalise objects and jump back,

E ducate people on Earth.

Paige Coleman (9)

St George's Primary School, Portland

Night Light

In the dark forest's embrace,
Where the tallest trees stand in grace,
Shadows stretch across the land,
As if held by a giant's hand.
Deeper into the woods we tread,
Mindful of what lies ahead.
With every step, a world unfolds,
Secrets waiting to be told.
Amongst the trees, whispers rise,
Nature's tales in silent guise.
Bouncing peas and talking trees,
Enchantment carried on the breeze.
Then, from heavens high above,
Descends a creature, filled with love.
The glimmering glowerfly,
Dancing beneath the twilight sky.
Swiftly, it flits out of view,
But caught by a friend, the moment grew.
In its light,
I draw a scene,
A moment captured, serene.

Yet as it departs, a curious sound,
A distant echo, strange and profound.
With a final flutter, it bids adieu,
Leaving us with a mysterious moo.

Jeron Harrison (10)
Woodhouse Primary Academy, Quinton

A Nightmare To Remember

I wake up in the woods, scared and alone
But the only thing beside me I see is a bone
The trees twist and tangle in the sky
The canopy seems like it's oh so high.

I take my first step being drenched in sweat
But I'm not quite sure what I have met
I bump into something but it isn't a tree
But it is a figure, tall as can be.

I look up at the sky but all I see
Is a scary face looking down at me
I ran and ran as fast as I could
But I soon tripped over a piece of wood.

I wake up in my bed screaming and crying
But I am soon asleep and the scariness is dying.

Lilly Keenahan (11)
Woodhouse Primary Academy, Quinton

Untitled

In our Year Six classroom,
Each day's a new quest,
And our teacher is the guide leading the best.
They weave numbers into tales
And make words dance,
Turning the ordinary into a magical chance.
Patience is their superpower,
Making challenges feel light,
And with a sprinkle of wisdom,
They make learning take flight.

In science experiments or language arts delight,
Our teacher's enthusiasm makes everything bright.
Year Six is a journey with our mentor so fine,
Shaping young minds like a craftsman of time.

Rawnaq Azad (10)
Woodhouse Primary Academy, Quinton

The Journey Of Life

One day we start as a little baby,
On earth, we think our mum is the only lady,
Being so small gets us so much love,
We're so spoiled, we can't even bother to look above.

Growing bigger every day, we start to walk,
We learn to talk and draw with chalk,
Day by day, we become more massive,
Somehow, we become more aggressive.

Time goes so fast, how did I graduate from school?
Now I'm starting to think that everyone is a fool,
Then we get a full-time job,
I have wrinkles, that's pretty odd.

Sagaa Abo Arida (11)
Woodhouse Primary Academy, Quinton

The Sea Tiger

A tiger with a fin,
A fin super thin,
In the sea it swims,
It swims and grins,
Its favourite dish is jellyfish jelly,
Since it knows it will fill its belly.

So you might be asking,
"What is it called?"
This mystical creature of old,
Is unlike anything ever spoken of.

The name is very strange (and very old),
But is fitting for a creature so bold,
As fluid as a fish,
As strong as a fighter,
The name of this creature is
The sea tiger.

Joseph Clerkin (10)
Woodhouse Primary Academy, Quinton

Behind The Door

Behind the door, the dragon listens,
Behind the door, the river glistens,
Behind the wooden, creaky door,
A fairy tale unfolds once more.

Behind the dragon, the fairies fly,
Behind the dragon is a wonderful night sky,
Behind the dragon, the jewels of the night shine bright,
As bright as the land of the light.

Behind the fairies, the goblins sneer,
Behind the fairies, the mermaids cheer,
Behind the fairies, the trees stand tall,
As tall as the Giants by Hadrian Wall.

Behind the goblins, the castle stood,
Behind the goblins was the deep, dark wood,
Behind the goblins, the siren sings,
And the pegasus flies with its beautiful wings.

In the castle, the princess sleeps,
In the castle, she wonders who she'll meet.
In the castle, she dreams all day,
Then she meets a girl called May.

In her dreams, May swims deep with the whales in the
sea,
In her dreams, May runs away from a dragon until she
is free,
In her dreams, May flies a carpet high in the sky,
And then goes on a secret mission as a spy.

Behind this dream is something the princess believes,
Behind this dream is a message we receive,
Behind this dream, the message is to let your
imagination run free,
You can't be wrong with creativity.

Ella Dyce (10)
Woolton Primary School, Woolton

The Dragon King Rises

Buried in the sand below,
The creature bellows and screams full of frustration.
Waiting for the correct time to arrive,
There he lies; broken down in pieces.

He has waited for years;
And now the Dragon King will surely rise.
After the victims escaped their destiny,
It would become: "The dragon's lucky..."

The dragon breathed his fire hard and loud,
Waiting for a peep of sound.
Finally, the people's homes are found
Now the dragon is down.

He lies under once again,
Waiting for the next victims.
He waits long and hard,
Where nobody will expect him...
He will pop out!

There he lies, full of despair,
Waiting for the next pair.
There he lies, waiting to the end;
Patiently staying until it is time.

They say it's over,
But it will never be completed.
They sometimes say he's hiding
Where they don't expect him to...

Yu Chen Xu (10)
Woolton Primary School, Woolton

Lost In A Magic Land

Her wings shone bright
In the midsummer night
A ship sailed across the sea in pursuit of her magic
The next part is tragic.

Captured, she was put in a tall glass
The captain screamed, "Avast!"
Tears rolled down her face
As she plotted her escape.

But this tale ends well
For the tall glass fell.
She whispered, "Hooray!"
And she shines bright to this day.

Sadie Weeks (10)
Woolton Primary School, Woolton

YOUNG WRITERS INFORMATION

We hope you have enjoyed reading this book – and that you will continue to in the coming years.

If you're a young writer who enjoys reading and creative writing, or the parent of an enthusiastic poet or story writer, do visit our website **www.youngwriters.co.uk**. Here you will find free competitions, workshops and games, as well as recommended reads, a poetry glossary and our blog.

If you would like to order further copies of this book, or any of our other titles, then please give us a call or visit **www.youngwriters.co.uk**.

Young Writers
Remus House
Coltsfoot Drive
Peterborough
PE2 9BF
(01733) 890066
info@youngwriters.co.uk